ISBN 978-0-9958208-2-1

All rights reserved. Published by Megan Olynyk
RR4, Calmar, Alberta, Canada, T0C0V0

This book is dedicated to my girls
Brynn, Ellie, Mallie and Bethany!

You are the inspiration to follow this dream!

I love you!

A Lamb Named Chicken
Farmyard Friends

written by Megan Olynyk | illustrated by Sara Dudenhoeffer

There was a chill in the air that morning. Fall had grown crisp and there was a touch of winter frost on the tips of the still green grass. Chicken the lamb enjoyed his morning grain and water and was excited to play with his best friend Duke, the Great Dane. Chicken and Duke played together everyday and had been best friends since Chicken first came to the farm.

While looking for Duke that morning, Chicken bumped into a laying hen named Nugget.

Nugget had just seen Duke in the pasture with Finnegan, the farm pony.

Chicken hurried over to the pasture where he could see that Duke and Finnegan were having a playful game of tag. Focused on their game of tag, Duke and Finnegan didn't notice Chicken was watching them play. After watching for a few minutes, Chicken felt sad, and he slowly returned to his pen.

That afternoon, Duke asked Chicken if he would like to play hide and seek in the barn with Fuzzpaw, the farm cat, and Sniffles, the bunny. Chicken was disappointed. He had hoped Duke would ask him to play one of their favorite games: toss the bottle, chase the car, or bury the bone.

Chicken and Duke always had fun playing together, but Chicken wasn't sure it would be fun playing hide and seek with Fuzzpaw and Sniffles.

Chicken decided to stay in his pasture to graze. Duke told him he would be in the barn if Chicken changed his mind.

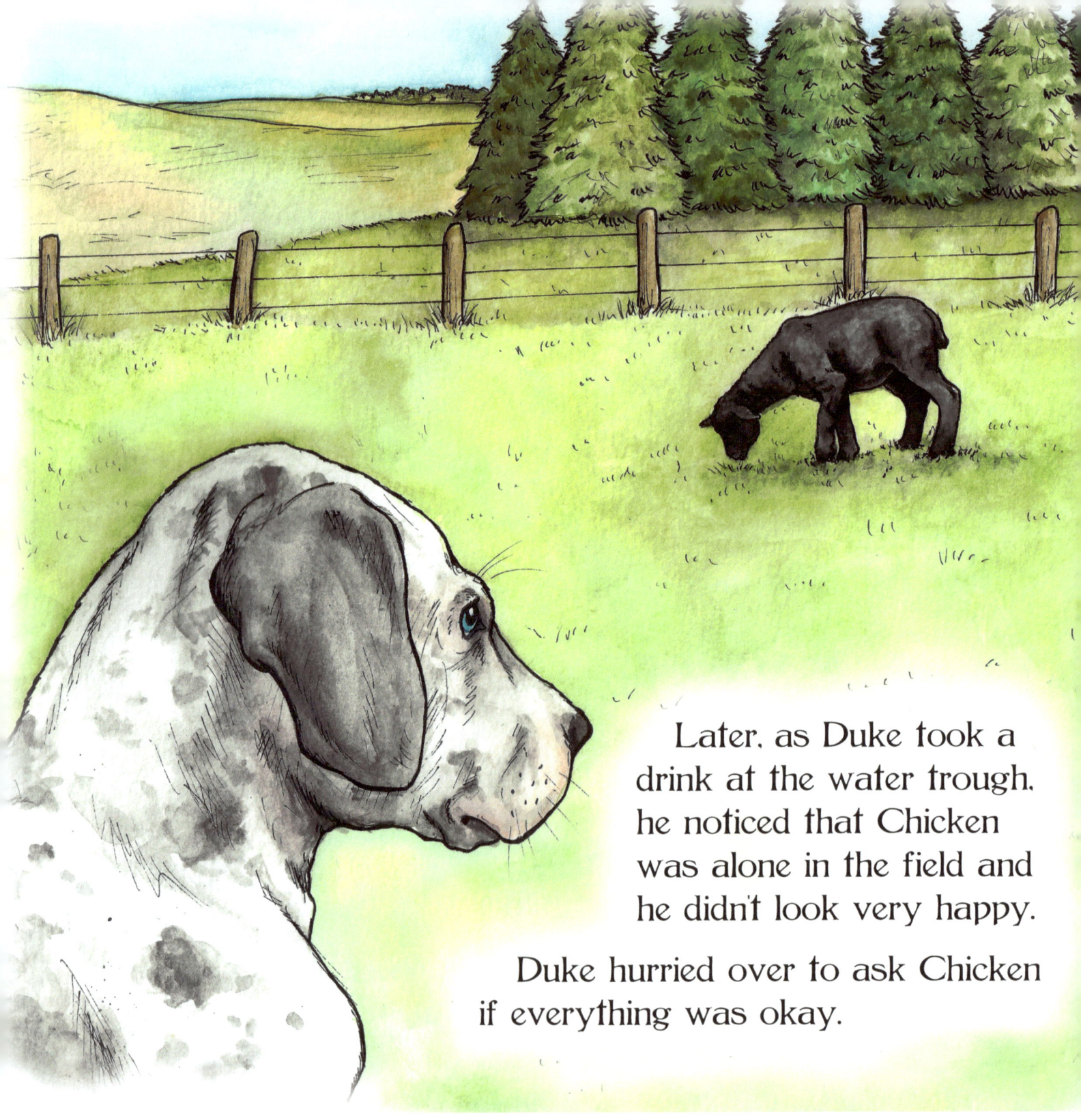

Later, as Duke took a drink at the water trough, he noticed that Chicken was alone in the field and he didn't look very happy.

Duke hurried over to ask Chicken if everything was okay.

Chicken asked Duke why he would play with Finnegan, Fuzzpaw and Sniffles if they were best friends. Chicken was worried that Duke didn't want to be best friends anymore.

This surprised Duke!

Duke told Chicken not to worry because they would always be best friends. Then Duke remembered that Fuzzpaw and Sniffles were still hiding in the barn, and headed off to find them.

After talking to Duke, Chicken still didn't feel any better. If they were best friends, why did Duke need to play with the other animals on the farm? Chicken went to bed feeling confused and uneasy. He had a tough time settling in for sleep.

When Chicken the Lamb woke the next morning. Duke was snuggled in beside him. There was a fresh blanket of snow covering the yard. It was so cold that Chicken could see his breath in the air. Chicken felt the winter chill on his face and was grateful for Duke's warm snuggles.

After breakfast, Duke and Chicken went for a walk around the farm. Duke took Chicken to the hen pen, where they saw Nugget and her best friend Wanda. Nugget and Wanda became friends when they were young hens. Wanda had somehow gotten her leg stuck under a watering can. Nugget had come along and helped Wanda free her leg. Now, the best friends have side by side egg laying pens and always lay their eggs at the same time of day.

Next, Duke and Chicken went to the barn. Dairy the cow was sharing some of her left over fresh milk with her best friend Fuzzpaw, the farm cat. Dairy and Fuzzpaw had been friends since Fuzzpaw was a kitten. Fuzzpaw had fallen asleep on top of Dairy's rickety old hay feeder. Dairy had spent that whole day making sure that Fuzzpaw didn't fall off the feeder and get hurt. Now Dairy has a special and safe place on her back where Fuzzpaw takes her naps.

Lastly, Duke and Chicken went to visit Finnegan and Sniffles, the oldest friends on the farm. Finnegan had been the first pet to come live on the farm and so had been quite lonely at first. One hot summer afternoon, a storm rolled in, spooking Finnegan. He ran through the field and almost stepped on little Sniffles hiding in the long grass. They decided to spend the rest of the storm together in the safety of the field shelter. Finnegan called his new friend 'Sniffles' because the wild bunny had gotten a runny nose from the cold storm. They had been best friends ever since.

Chicken was enjoying his morning walk with Duke, but he wasn't sure why they had gone to see everyone. He already knew that each of these pairs were best friends.

Chicken laid down under his favorite tree and began to understand. Yesterday, when Chicken came upon the other farm animals, they were not playing with their best friends. Then, that morning, all of the animals were with their best friends doing the things they enjoyed.

Being best friends didn't mean that he and Duke had to play with only each other every day. They could be best friends and have other friends and fun too! All of the animals on the farm are friends, they can all play together, and they are all very lucky to have so many friends to have fun with!

That afternoon, after Chicken and Duke finished a game of toss and catch the bottle, Chicken the lamb, Duke the Great Dane, Nugget and Wanda the laying hens, Fuzzpaw the cat, Dairy the cow, Sniffles the bunny, and Finnegan the pony all played a game of kick the milk can. Chicken had fun, Duke had fun   it was fun for everyone!

Can you find...

Duke	Dairy	Fuzzpaw	a pigeon
Wanda	Finnegan	Chicken the Lamb	a shovel
Nugget	Sniffles	a hot air balloon	a wagon wheel